Cause
Effect
Chaos!

Rainforest

Author Paul Mason
with artwork by Mark Ruffle

Enslow PUBLISHING

The website addresses (URLs) included in this book were valid at the time of going to press. However, it is possible that contents or addresses may have changed since the publication of this book. No responsibility for any such change can be accepted by either the author or the Publisher.

Published in 2026 by Enslow Publishing, LLC
2544 Clinton Street
Buffalo, NY 14224

First published in Great Britain in 2018 by Wayland

Series editor: Paul Rockett
Series design and illustration: Mark Ruffle
www.rufflebrothers.com

Manufactured in the United States of America

CPSIA compliance information: Batch #CSENS26: For further information contact Enslow Publishing LLC, New York, New York at 1-800-398-2504.

Please visit our website, www.enslowpublishing.com. For a free color catalog of all our high-quality books, call toll free 1-800-398-2504 or fax 1-877-980-4454.

Cataloging-in-Publication Data
Names: Mason, Paul. | Ruffle, Mark, illustrator.
Title: Rainforest / Paul Mason ; illustrated by Mark Ruffle.
Description: Buffalo, NY : Enslow Publishing, 2026. |
Series: Cause, effect, chaos! | Includes glossary and index.
Identifiers: ISBN 9781978545359 (pbk.) | ISBN 9781978545366 (library bound) |
ISBN 9781978545373 (ebook)
Subjects: LCSH: Rain forests--Juvenile literature. | Rain forest ecology--Juvenile literature. Classification: LCC QH541.5.R26 M376 2026 | DDC 577.34--dc23

Contents

Cause and Effect

Why do events happen? Usually it's because of something else that happened before.

You'll definitely be able to come up with examples of this from your own life. Just imagine:

You beg and plead with your parents for a new skateboard.

Weeks of pressure finally have an effect:

a new skateboard!

Of course, the effect is not always good. Sometimes it's chaos!

Having the new skateboard inspires you to try some new tricks …

Rainforests are an important part of our world. What happens in them and the effects are important for all of us.

The rainforest is a massive tangle of causes and effects. For example:

Rain falls in the forest.

The water allows plants to grow and animals to drink.

Sometimes, though, the effect of an action is chaos:

People cut down the trees on a steep slope.

With no tree roots to keep the soil in place, a landslide happens.

Soaked!

You would expect a rainforest to be rainy. That's how it got its name, after all. But rainforests are not just wet. They are part of a system called the water cycle.

The cycle begins in the morning, when the sun comes up.

The sun heats the air and the forest becomes hot.

The forest's warm, wet air rises.

As it gets higher the air cools, and the water it contains forms clouds.

As the next day heats up, the warm, wet air rises to form clouds again.

If the temperature rises too much, though, less rain falls. If this happens often, parts of the rainforest dry out and disappear.

Disaster!

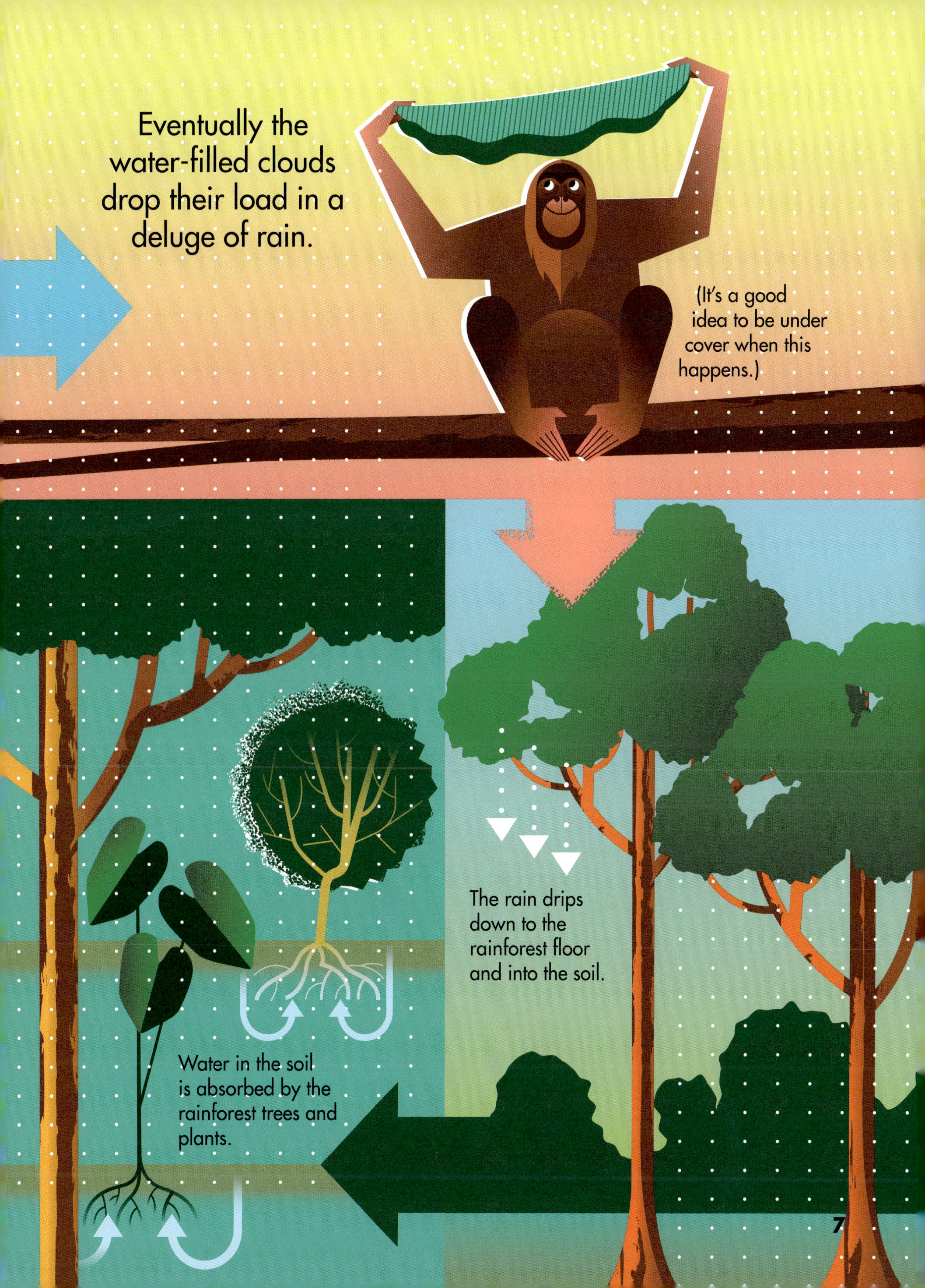

Eventually the water-filled clouds drop their load in a deluge of rain.

(It's a good idea to be under cover when this happens.)

The rain drips down to the rainforest floor and into the soil.

Water in the soil is absorbed by the rainforest trees and plants.

Raging Rivers

As well as from clouds formed close by, rainforests get water from clouds that have formed over the sea.

The Amazon rainforest, for example, gets extra water from clouds born over the Atlantic Ocean. And all that extra water has to go somewhere ...

When rain drips onto the forest floor some creeps downhill, creating small streams.

The streams feed rainforest rivers.

The biggest rainforest river, the Amazon, could fill about 2,000 swimming pools per second.

Small rivers feed into **bigger ones**, which flow toward the sea. A huge amount of water flows

downstream.

The power of flowing water can be used to make electricity, so hydroelectric dams are sometimes built on rainforest rivers.

When water from the dam is released it flows to the sea. The process begins again.

The dams flood large areas of forest. The plants, animals, and people that live there lose their home.

The Fight for Light

One crucial ingredient for a rainforest is rain. The other is (of course) trees.

In a tropical rainforest, the trees have to grow quickly. They need to escape the gloomy forest floor and reach life-giving sunshine as soon as possible.

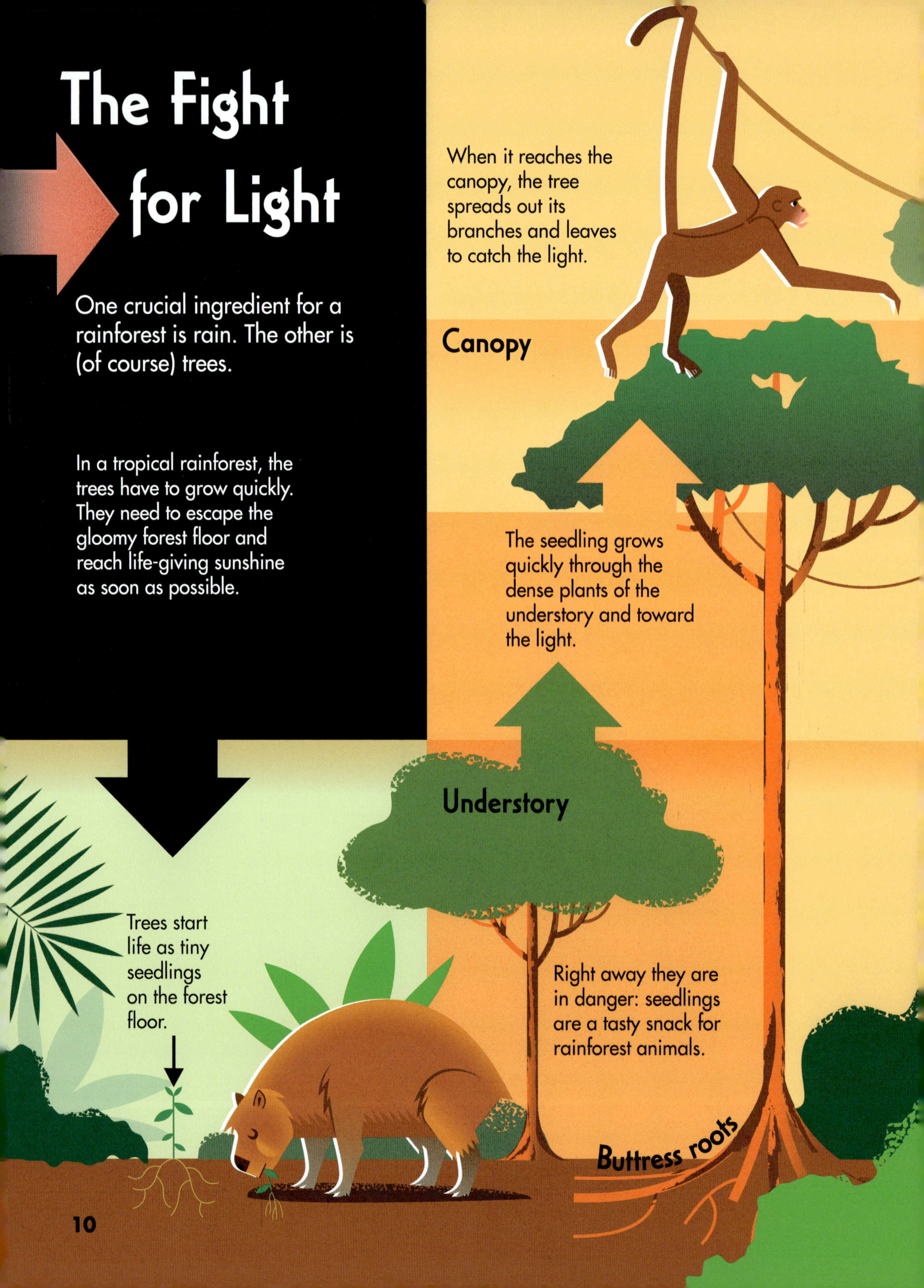

When it reaches the canopy, the tree spreads out its branches and leaves to catch the light.

The seedling grows quickly through the dense plants of the understory and toward the light.

Trees start life as tiny seedlings on the forest floor.

Right away they are in danger: seedlings are a tasty snack for rainforest animals.

Some trees keep on growing, into the clear air above the canopy.

Water is harder to get above the canopy, so in dry times the tallest trees shed their leaves to prevent water loss.

If the weather gets too dry, forest fires start.

Millions of rainforest trees a year are destroyed by fire, causing **chaos** for the animals who live there.

Look out Below!

When a new clearing appears in the rainforest, the Brazil nut tree has a clever process for making sure it fills the space.

The only trouble is, it can be a bit hazardous if you happen to be walking past at a crucial moment …

The Brazil nut tree produces seedpods. The pods are a long way up from the ground.

When the pods are ripe, they drop to the ground. They weigh the same as a small cannonball.

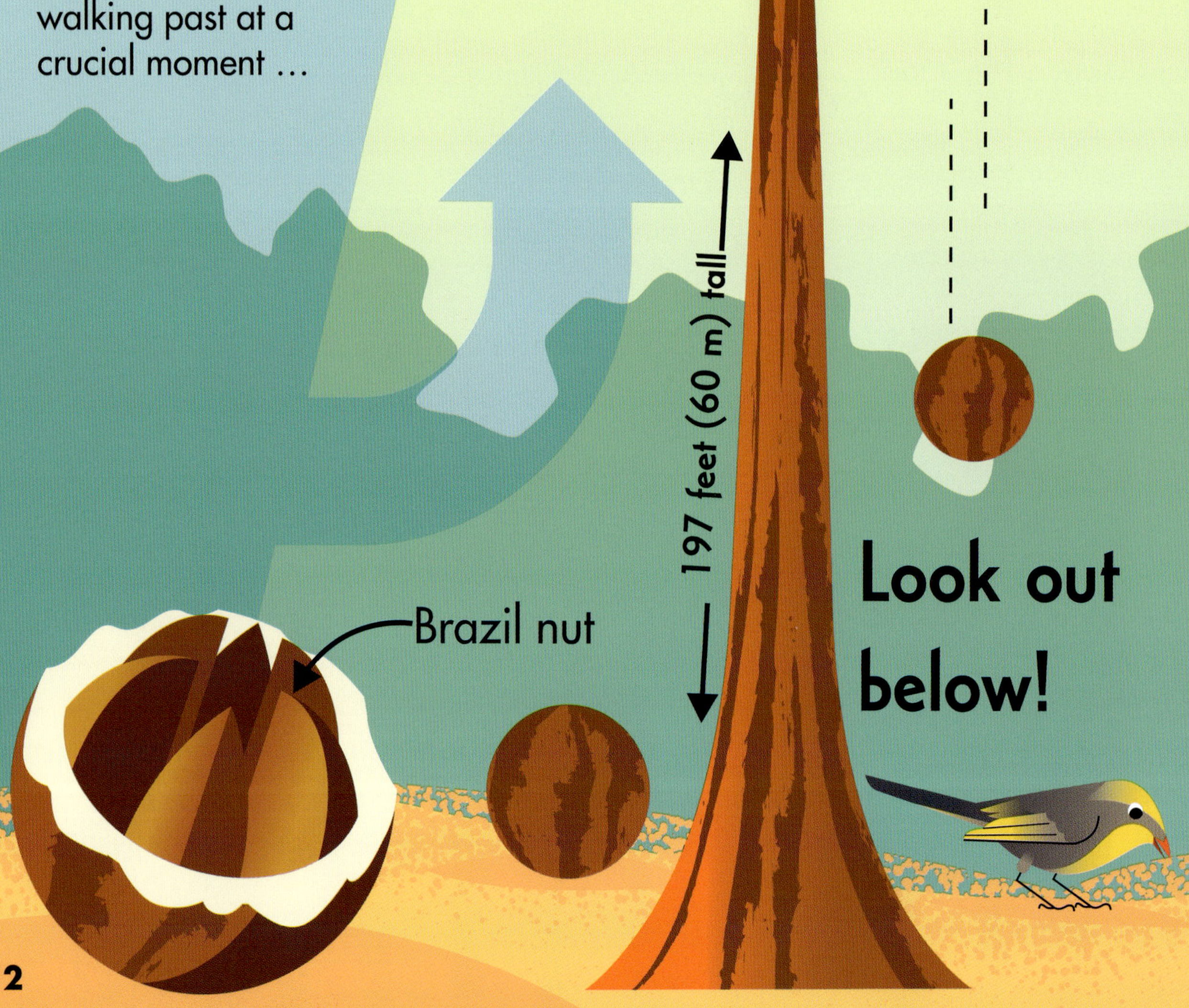

Look out below!

To survive the landing, the pods have to be really strong. Only the agouti has teeth that can chew through to the seeds inside.

The agouti eats some seeds and hides others for later. But sometimes agoutis forget where they put their seeds.

The seeds stay hidden for years, until a clearing appears above and sunlight reaches the forest floor.

The sunlight signals the seeds to start growing.

The seedlings have to grow fast. If the **sunlight** is blocked by other plants, they may not survive.

Piranha Danger!

Tropical rainforests are hot and sweaty. But anyone tempted to go for a swim to cool down should think twice! Predators lurk in the cloudy water.

Among the most famous is a fearsome little fish: the Amazonian piranha. But how does the piranha hunt?

If something plops into the water nearby, the piranhas sense it and investigate.

The most aggressive piranhas are black and red-bellied ones. They swim along in shoals of about 20.

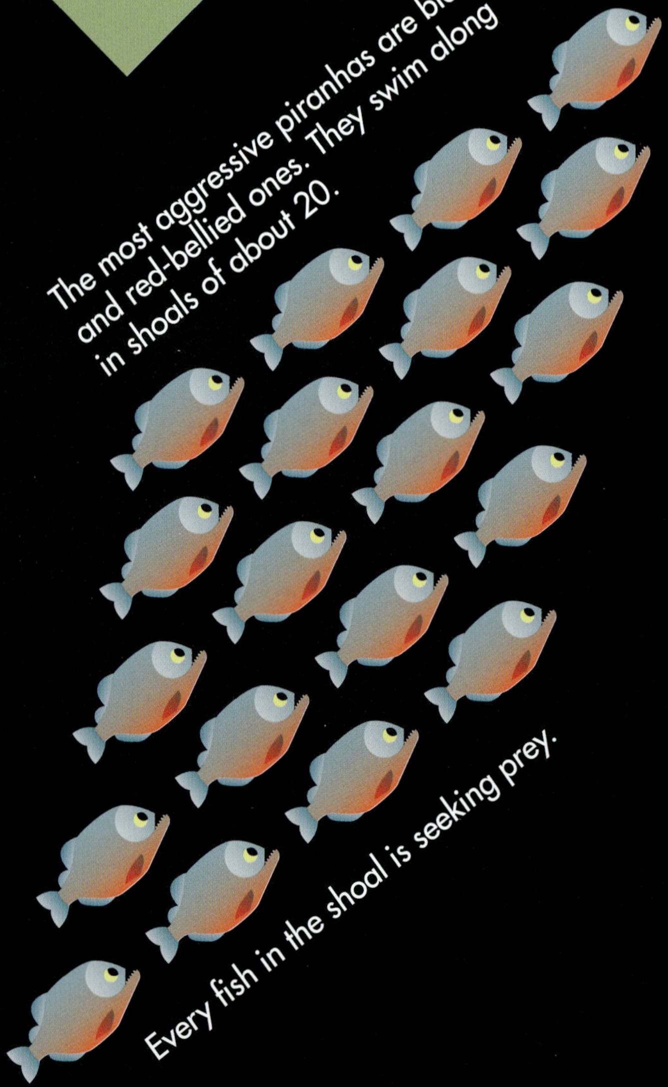

Every fish in the shoal is seeking prey.

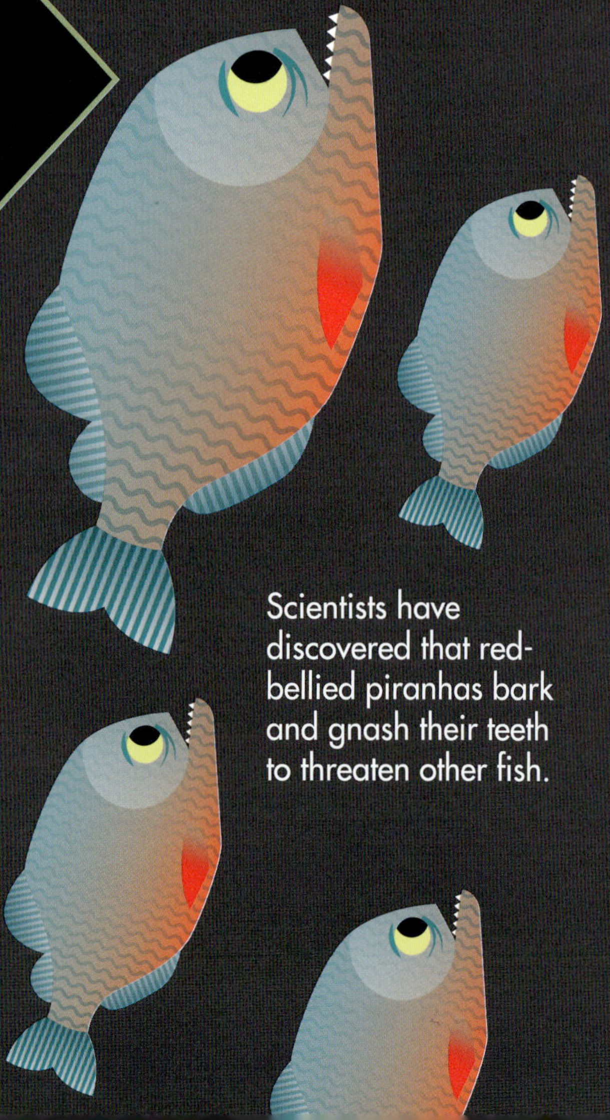

Scientists have discovered that red-bellied piranhas bark and gnash their teeth to threaten other fish.

If there is **blood** in the water, the piranhas smell it.

Piranhas can smell one drop of blood in a bathtub full of water, so a bleeding animal is like a sign for lunch.

The shoal attacks. Their sharp teeth bite into their prey.

The piranhas concentrate on the attack. They should watch out, though!

Piranhas' teeth often fall out or break. When this happens, new ones replace them.

Piranha is one of the spectacled caiman's favorite meals. A caiman could sneak up on them at any minute.

Ant Antics

In the rainforest, ants are everywhere. There are edible ants that taste like lemons, bullet ants whose bite is like being shot, and ferocious army ants that devour anything in their path.

There are also, of course, ordinary ants. Every ant in their colony has a job that's aimed at making sure the colony continues.

The colony's main need is food. Specialist scout ants set off across the forest floor, sniffing for anything edible.

When a scout **senses food**, it follows the smell to its source. Ants love sweet plant nectar.

Ants smell using their antennae.

When the scout finds nectar, it heads back to the colony. It lays a scent trail using chemicals called pheromones.

A column of worker ants sets out to collect the nectar. More and more ants follow the scent trail and climb into the plant. But it's **a trap!**

Since the scout visited, it has rained. The sides of the plant are slippery, so the ants cannot climb back out.

And this is a pitcher plant. **It's carnivorous!** The fluid in the bottom slowly melts the ants into ant soup, which the plant digests.

Tiger Alert!

Some of the world's biggest cats live in rainforests. The forests of South Asia are home to the biggest of all: the tiger.

Tigers are **apex predators**. They are at the top of the food chain. At the bottom of the chain are much smaller animals.

The plants are eaten by monkeys such as the lion-tailed macaque and deer such as the Indian muntjac.

The chain begins with plants, which grow quickly in the warm, wet forest.

Young deer are sometimes attacked and killed by Indian wild boar. Boar will eat almost anything, from fruit and nuts to snakes and lizards.

If they are eating young deer, the boars need to watch out for tigers. Tigers eat deer, as well as monkeys, birds, fish … and boar.

Nothing preys on tigers

–except humans. Every year, people kill hundreds of tigers.

So many have died that there is a risk tigers may become extinct.

Slash and Burn

Many people who live in rainforests grow their own food. To clear land for planting crops they use a system called slash and burn.

The slash-and-burn process usually starts during the driest part of the year.

First people chop down most of the plants and trees. They leave any that could provide food or timber.

The chopped-down vegetation is left to dry in the sun.

As the driest part of the year ends, it is set **aflame.**

As soon as the ashes have cooled, crops are planted. Rainforest soil does not contain many nutrients, and the ashes provide some extra ones.

The crops get plenty of water when the wet season starts. This and the extra nutrients mean they grow quickly.

As they grow, the crops use up the nutrients in the soil. After a year or two, these nutrients have gone and crops will not grow.

The people have to clear a new piece of land.

If too much land is cleared, the soil never recovers. Trees cannot grow and part of the rainforest **disappears forever.**

First Contact

A hundred years ago, few people from outside came to rainforests. Today though, settlers, loggers, miners, and others are moving in.

When outsiders arrive, they make "first contact" with undiscovered tribes–often with catastrophic results.

For example, newcomers arrived when a road was built into the territory of the Paraná people in Brazil.

The Paraná came out of the forest to meet the strangers. Some of the newcomers had brought with them diseases such as colds, flu, and measles.

The Paraná caught the new diseases. They had not experienced them before and had no immunity.

Roughly half the Paraná quickly died. The government airlifted the survivors to new lands, away from the road.

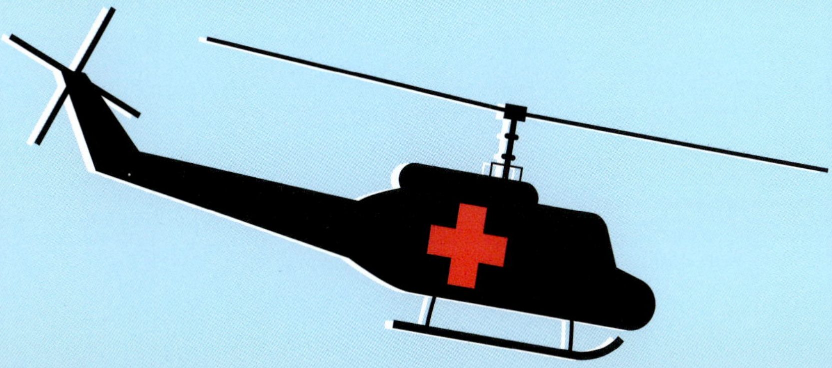

The deaths continued in the new lands.

In the end, 80 percent of the tribe died.

Twenty years after they had been forced to leave, the remaining Paraná returned to their homeland.

Orangutan Orphans

Rainforest soil is not ideal for growing crops, but one that does grow well is oil palm.

The oil is used in thousands of products: foods, soaps, and cosmetics. But oil palm plantations cause problems for the rainforest plants and animals–including orangutans.

During the land clearance, big animals such as tigers, elephants, and orangutans, are killed to get them out of the way.

If the animals have young, these are killed or sold as pets. Baby orangutans can be

sold for hundreds of dollars.

Before planting oil palms, the farmers clear the rainforest of other trees and plants.

In Indonesia and Malaysia, clearing land for oil palm plantations is now the biggest cause of

forest destruction.

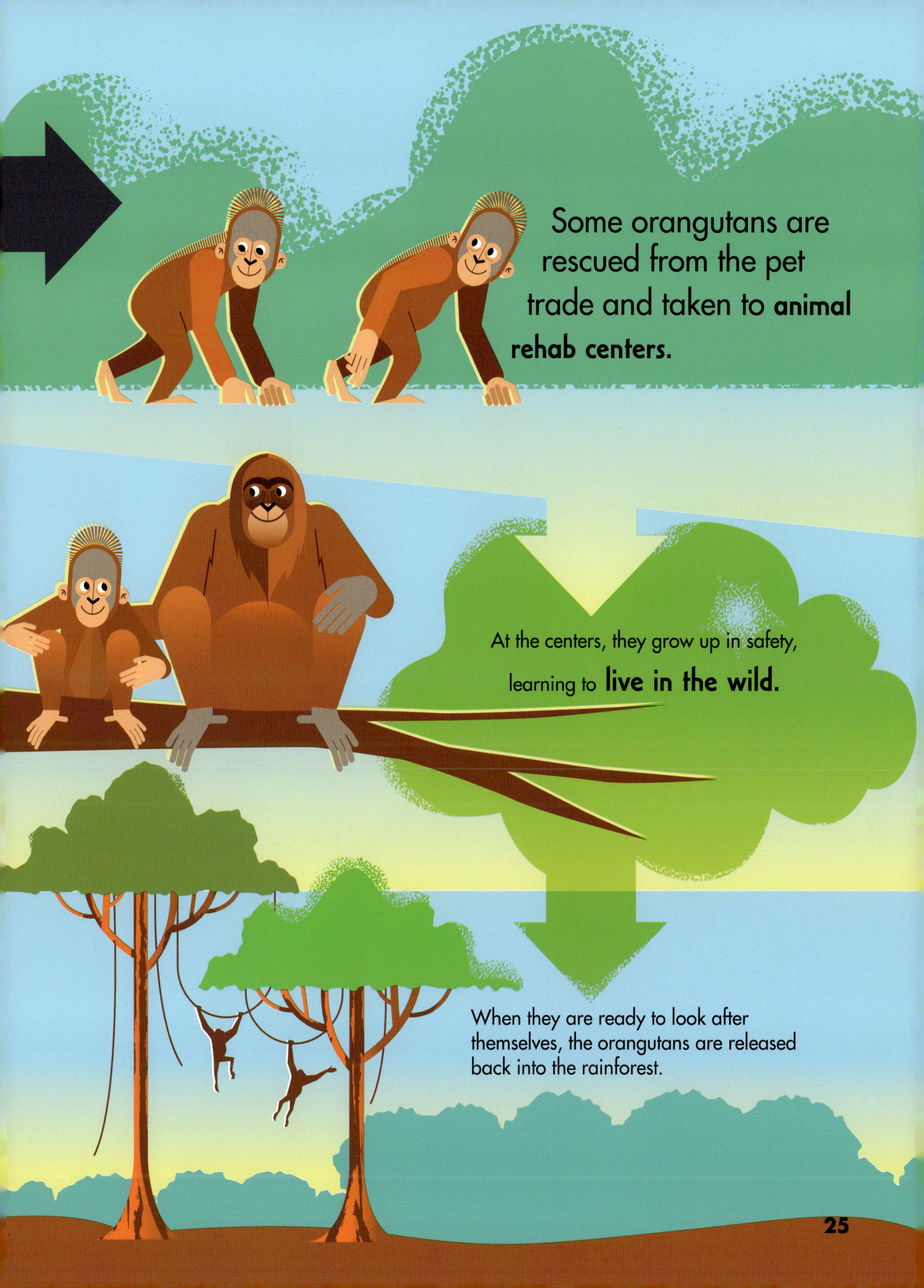

Some orangutans are rescued from the pet trade and taken to **animal rehab centers.**

At the centers, they grow up in safety, learning to **live in the wild.**

When they are ready to look after themselves, the orangutans are released back into the rainforest.

Forest Gold

The riverbanks and beaches of the Amazon contain gold. It washed downriver from the Andes mountains centuries ago.

Today, thousands of gold prospectors are at work in the Amazon. They are causing big problems in the rainforest.

Mercury, a liquid metal, is added to the barrels. It picks up any remaining bits of gold, which are then removed.

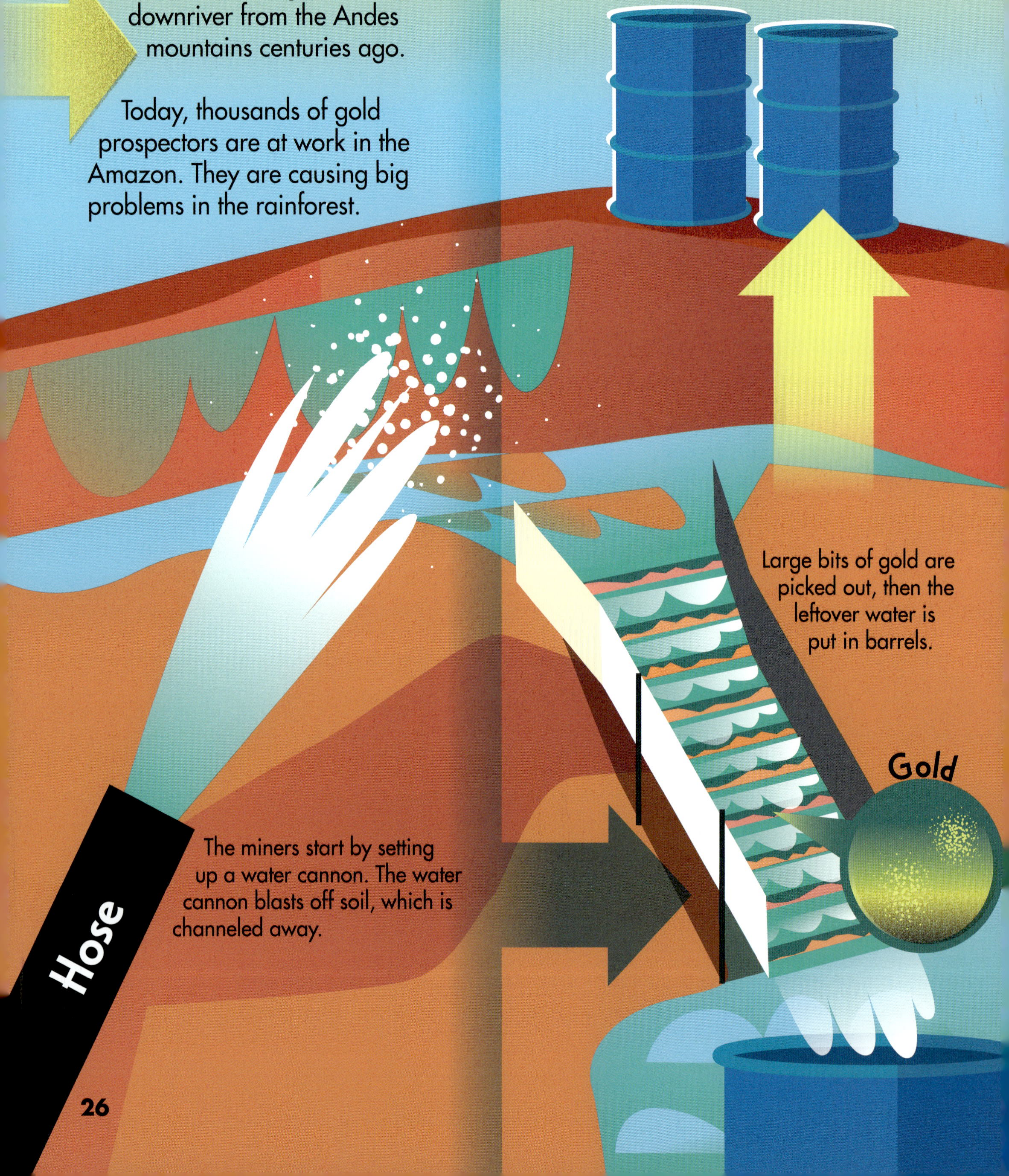

Large bits of gold are picked out, then the leftover water is put in barrels.

The miners start by setting up a water cannon. The water cannon blasts off soil, which is channeled away.

The water, which still contains mercury, is tipped into nearby rivers.

Small fish absorb some of the mercury.

Big fish, birds, and caimans eat a lot of smaller fish, so they collect a lot of mercury.

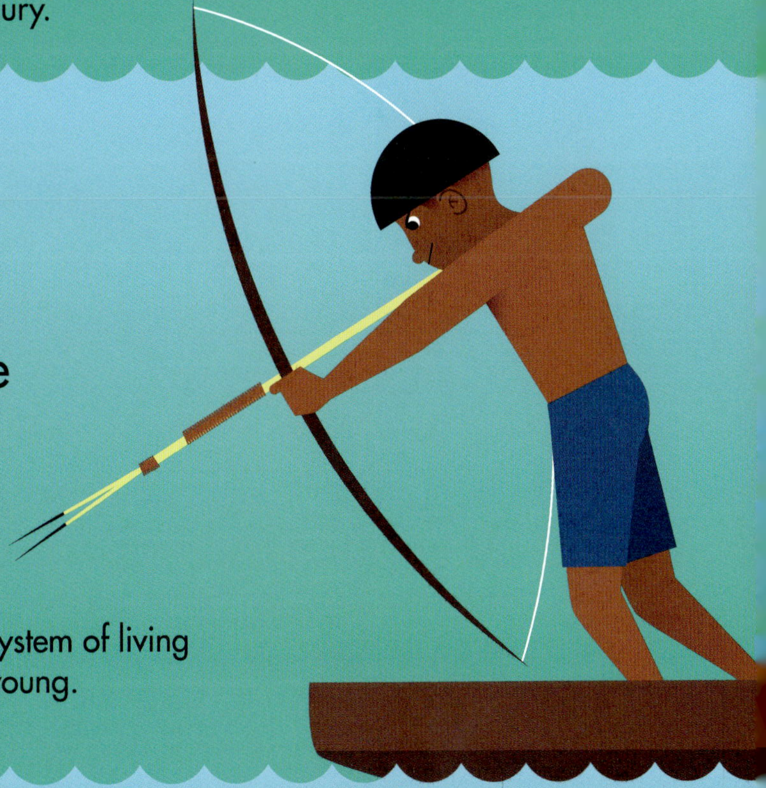

People living nearby catch and eat the fish–as well as the mercury they contain.

Mercury damages the central nervous system of living creatures. It also causes harm to their unborn young.

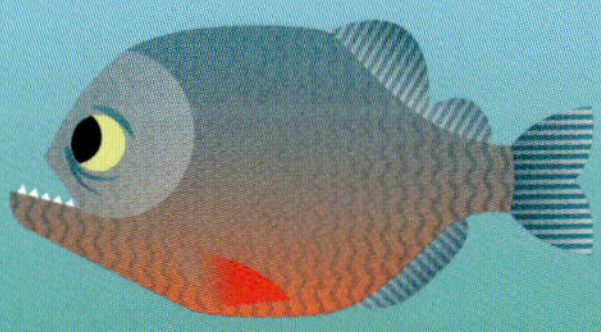

Tim-ber!

The world's rainforests are shrinking. Their trees are cut down to sell the timber, or to clear land for farming.

Cutting down rainforests causes damage to the environment everywhere on Earth.

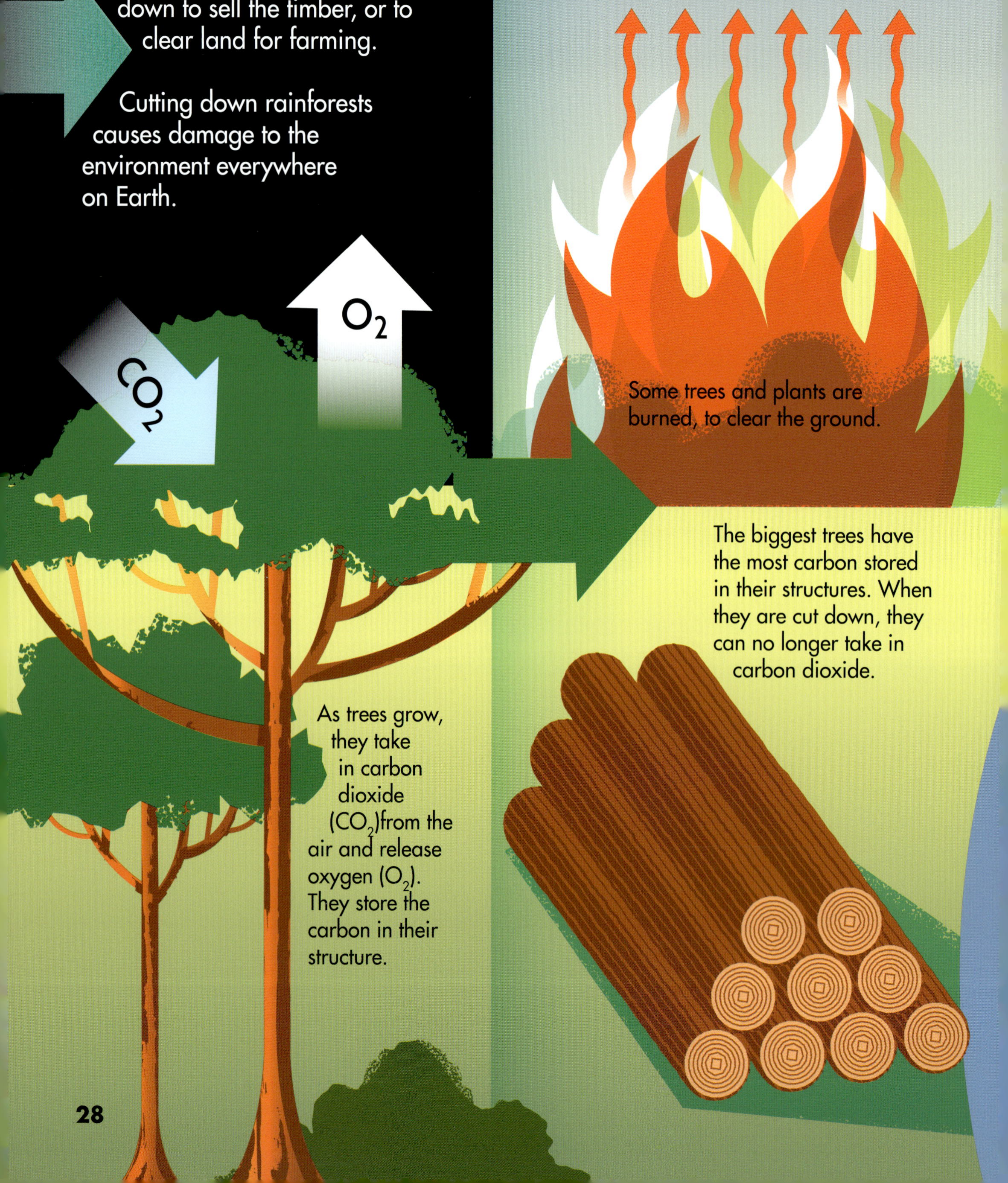

As trees grow, they take in carbon dioxide (CO_2) from the air and release oxygen (O_2). They store the carbon in their structure.

The biggest trees have the most carbon stored in their structures. When they are cut down, they can no longer take in carbon dioxide.

Some trees and plants are burned, to clear the ground.

The carbon they contain is released into the atmosphere as carbon dioxide.

The carbon dioxide rises into the atmosphere, where it joins a layer of greenhouse gases. This layer stops heat from escaping into space.

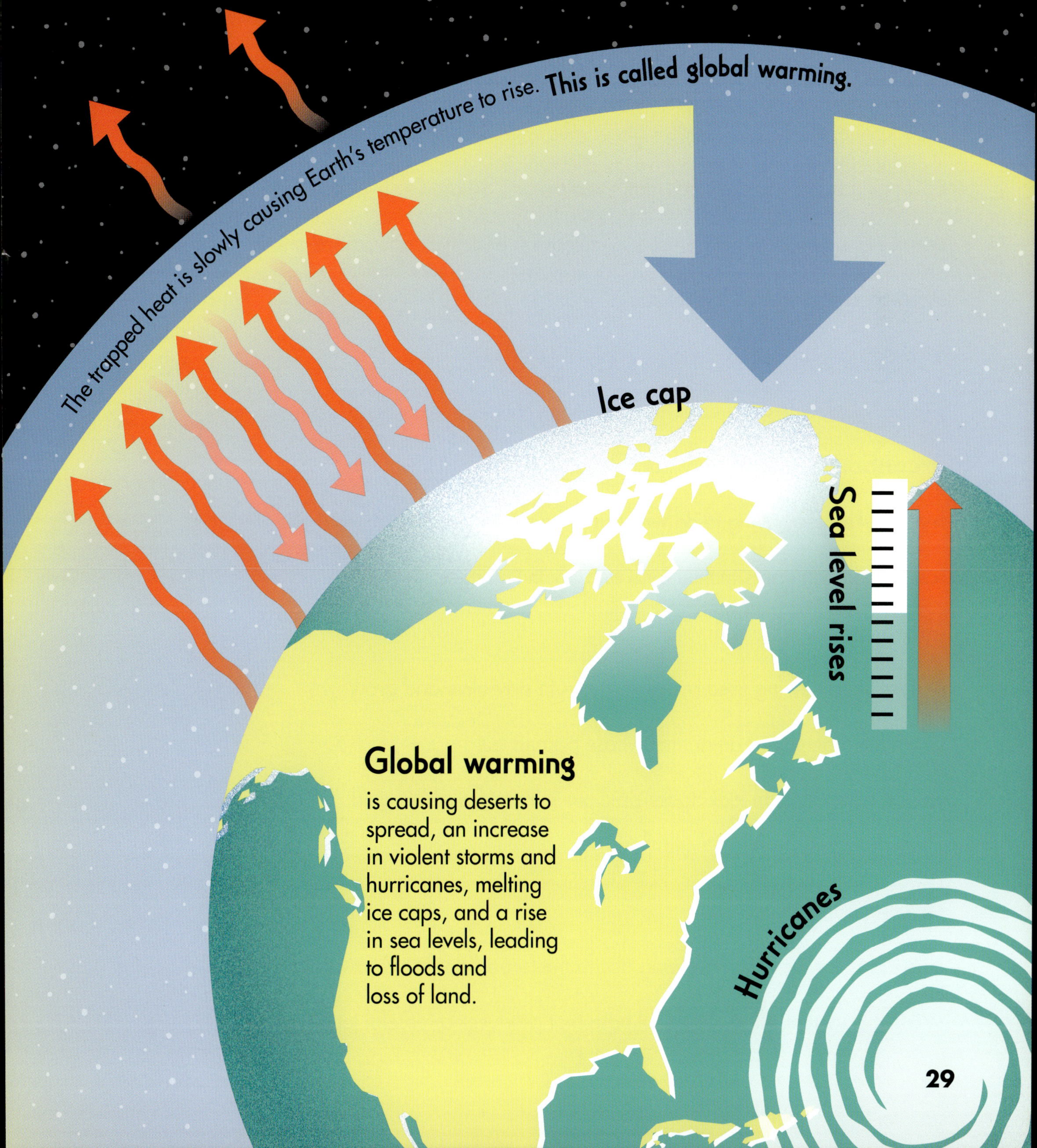

Global warming

is causing deserts to spread, an increase in violent storms and hurricanes, melting ice caps, and a rise in sea levels, leading to floods and loss of land.

Glossary

airlifted taken somewhere in a helicopter or airplane

apex predator animal at the top of the food chain. It is not hunted by other animals in its natural environment.

canopy the top layer of leaves and branches in a forest

central nervous system network of nerves that controls a body's movement. In animals with a backbone, the core of the central nervous system is the brain and spinal column.

colony group of living things that has moved to an area to live there

cosmetics beauty products used to improve a person's appearance or create an image

deluge sudden fall of a lot of rain

extinct no longer in existence; completely died out

global warming increase in the average temperature of Earth's atmosphere

greenhouse gas gas that traps warmth in Earth's atmosphere

hydroelectric having to do with using the movement of water to make electricity

ice cap frozen areas at the North and South Poles

immunity ability to resist a disease

nutrient something used by living things to stay alive and grow

orphan a person or an animal whose parents died

prospector person looking for precious minerals, such as gold

plantation area planted with all the same kind of trees or other crop

shoal group of fish

understory the plants growing above the forest floor but below the canopy

water cannon large, powerful hose that produces a forceful jet of water

Finding out more

Books

Conaghan, Bernard. *The Amazing Rainforest.* Coral Springs, FL: Seahorse Publishing, 2025.

Mather, Charis. *Tropical Rainforest Food Webs.* Buffalo, NY: KidHaven Publishing, 2024.

O'Brien, Cynthia. *Endangered Animals of the Rainforest.* Minneapolis, MN: Kaleidoscope, 2025.

Websites

Rainforest Habitat
https://kids.nationalgeographic.com/nature/habitats/article/rain-forest
Check out pictures and facts about the rainforest habitat.

What Is a Rainforest Habitat?
https://www.bbc.co.uk/bitesize/articles/zwkfrmn
Explore the rainforest!

Index